A Beginners Guide

into

CRYSTAL HEALING

BY
ROBERT W. WOOD D.HP
(Diploma in Hypnotherapy)

oOo

Including an adult section
of
Gemstones and Crystals

Rosewood Publishing

First Published in the U.K. 2014
By Rosewood Publishing
59 Croft Gardens
Birkby
Huddersfield
West Yorkshire
HD2 2FL
UK

www.rosewood-gifts.co.uk

Email:- info@rosewood-gifts.co.uk

All rights reserved. © 2014
No part of this book may be reproduced or utilised in any form or by any means, electronic or mechanical, including photocopying, recording or by any information storage and retrieval system, without permission in writing from the publisher.

Robert W Wood D.Hp
Asserts the moral right to be identified
as the Author of this work.

Cover photograph by
Andrew Caveney BA (Hons)
www.andrewcaveneyphotography.co.uk

ISBN 978-0-9567913-4-4   BK15

Exploring the Mystical World of Gemstones and Crystals.

Introduction
When it comes to crystal healing, it's true to say that there are divided opinions. These range from the total non-believers to those who do believe, leaving the majority of us firmly in the middle, not knowing what to believe. The author of this book started out thinking it would probably all be nonsense, just like having fairies at the bottom of the garden. (Sorry, if you believe in fairies). But I quickly learned it might not be nonsense, and in fact I now firmly believe that for many, under certain circumstances, crystal healing actually does seem to work.

Everybody's heard stories about crystal healing. There was the woman who was given a crystal to help her bad knee and then found, to her amazement, that her knee miraculously got better. Or people who can't sleep, who find that placing an Amethyst under their pillow seems to make them sleep like logs. Would you believe headaches can just seem to vanish? That'll be a Rose Quartz. Women becoming pregnant after years of trying – ask them how, and they may say it was a Moonstone. Eyesight improving – that'll be Obsidian Snowflake. Memory improving – Rhodonite. Need to boost your confidence? – then try a Tiger's Eye, a beautiful stone from South Africa.

You could bring back the joys of spring with a Sodalite; and if you place a Sodalite with a Rhodonite in a glass of water, it produces the 'Elixir of Life', said to rejuvenate and produce youthfulness. Aches and pains? Then what you need is a Rose Quartz and Hematite combined. It's said they work wonders on aches and pains. Maybe you would like a little 'Peace of Mind'? Then try green Aventurine, Rose Quartz and Rhodonite. Not feeling too good? Then the 'Healer' could be just what the doctor ordered: Carnelian, Red Jasper and Rock Crystal. And there are many more, so whatever the problem, there'll be a crystal that can help.

A Beginners Guide into Crystal Healing

This book has been written to help those who are interested in alternative treatments, treatments without side-effects that drugs can have. It's for those who can enjoy the feeling of being connected, or are just curious about gemstones and crystals. However, common sense should tell you to see your doctor or practitioner first, before embarking on any kind of alternative treatment. The information that follows is in direct response to those that would like to more, and is part of a series of books called 'Power for Life – a growing series of books based on the mysteries surrounding gemstones and crystals; a refreshing view of an ancient wisdom. Keep an open mind and you won't go far wrong.

If you thought Gemstones and Crystals were just lumps of rocks, you're in for a pleasant surprise. They are nature's little treasures, and have been around for a very long time. In fact they have been around as long as time itself, and a lot longer than any chemists.

Crystal Healing
Crystals and Gemstones have always been highly prized, not only because of their colour or beauty but also for their healing and spiritual properties. Science has yet to discover what actually occurs during crystal healing, and yet this in no way diminishes the fact that real changes are clearly felt by many. Placing a crystal close to an energy imbalance (an illness), whether it's physical or emotional, seems to encourage our own healing process to become activated.

The Sages, very often the High Priests, were revered for their profound wisdom and knowledge. They were also regarded as the 'medical practitioners' of their time. Without the advantages of our modern knowledge and drugs, they had to discover and use more natural remedies for healing the sick. Their skills must have seemed astounding to their people. They had to rely entirely on natural elements to effect their cures and bring about relief for many kinds of illness.

These 'wise men' were drawn to crystals, maybe because of their colour, purity or even shape, but obviously felt that crystals had special powers. In today's frantic, stressful and busy world, many people are seeking an alternative lifestyle.

A Beginner's Guide into Crystal Healing

Many are turning once again back to Mother Nature and the mineral kingdom, to see if they can discover the healing properties of crystals for themselves. This is one explanation for the upsurge in the number of people wanting to know more, and the reason behind the popularity of the many 'crystal healing workshops'.

By simply holding or wearing a crystal, or even just being near to one, people have often found a long-lasting beneficial effect; a feeling of calm, of being less agitated, of being energised, revitalised, and in many cases even completely healed. According to the holistic healers, when we are ill we are out of balance with nature, and a crystal, being pure and energised with the power of the earth and the power that created it, can help to guide us back into balance. A little like if a radio station goes off station; what do we do? We retune it in, until it's in tune, back on station. In our case, we're brought back into health.

It's exactly the same as the explanation given for swimming with dolphins: just being near a dolphin can, for many, have amazing beneficial effects.

What are Crystals?
Earth was formed around 4,500 million years ago, and all the building blocks of the Universe are captured here on earth. Our earth is over 80% 'crystal', the crust being elements – Sodium, Aluminium, Calcium, Iron, Magnesium and Potassium – this 'chemical cocktail' helped to produce the building blocks for our world. With this cocktail came an amazing variety of Gemstones and Crystals in all kinds of shapes, sizes and colours.

Crystals are of mineral substance, and their molecular composition is arranged and geometrically fixed. When you look at a crystal you can see many different sides or 'faces', angles, planes and points. The word 'crystal' comes from the Greek word 'krystallos' meaning 'ice'. The Greeks gave the name believing that crystals were ice, frozen. Crystalline materials as diverse as sugar, metal, salt – even our teeth- have all got one thing in common: an ordered internal structure of a regularly-repeating three-dimensional pattern.

Even the most irregular or misshapen crystal shares this atomical neatness. A crystal's external shape is dependent on its specific chemical ingredients, the way the atoms are linked together, and the conditions prevailing at the time of growth. There are many different permutations, producing a wide variation in shapes, colour and hardness.

Colour
The majority of crystals contain 'rogue' atoms – minute impurities, usually metal, within their chemical structure. These trace elements, or impurities, contribute to the wide range of colours. As a general rule of thumb: the greater the amount of trace impurities contained within the crystal, the deeper the colour. There are some crystals, such as agate and jasper, which we call Gemstones. These contain the same atomic structure, but, unlike crystal, their form is not visible to the naked eye and they appear to be ordinary coloured stones without geometric form, just like pebbles from a beach. Only by using a microscope is it possible to see the thousands of little crystals of which they are composed.

Crystal electricity
Certain crystals, most notably the Quartz family, can convert mechanical pressure into electrical energy. To demonstrate this, take two quartz crystals – rock crystal, rose quartz or amethyst will do – and rub them together in the dark. You'll see them light up quite spectacularly. It's called a 'piezoelectric' effect, from the Greek word 'piezo' meaning 'I press'. If you have a gas oven you may have used a special lighter-wand to create a spark. This special tool has a piece of quartz built into it, which releases energy (the spark) when it is used and works without the need of a battery. While natural quartz is abundant, it is rarely perfect, with all its 'rogue' trace elements rendering it unsuitable for commercial use. That is why piezoelectric crystals are produced synthetically in the laboratory. Although synthetic, they still have the same atomic structure and properties as their natural counterparts.

From Science to the 'mysteries'
Even earliest man found gemstones and crystals attractive and colourful, and used them for jewellery; but at the same time there was another interest developing, and this more to do with their 'magical attraction', rather than their looks.

It's not difficult to understand their fascination, when you think about the piezoelectric effect stones that light up.

I think it's strange that even to-day, things don't seem to have changed that much. On one hand we have the geologists, who will drool over a lovely piece of crystal and talk about its shape, its symmetry, its inclusions and how it looks. On the other hand, we have the New Age followers – crystal healers and the alternative therapists – all drooling over the same piece and explaining how it feels, describing its energy, its power and what it can do

A Quartz Watch
Scientific research has shown an amazing fact: that crystals vibrate at different frequencies. For example, a digital watch works because a small piece of quartz vibrates at a constant frequency when stimulated by the energy from a battery.

Why is there a quartz in a watch? The answer is, because quartz makes a timepiece so accurate, to within only a second or two a year – and that's accurate. So how does it work? Scientists discovered that the atoms within a micro-thin slice of synthetic quartz (such as is ideal for clocks and watches) vibrate at 32,768 times per second. The crystal requires very little power, and this is often supplied by a very tiny battery. As the atoms in the quartz vibrate they emit very precise electronic pulses. Theses pulses are then channelled through microchip circuitry, where they are successively halved in a series of 15 steps. The result is really astounding: it produces a single, constant pulse per second. Which is why watches and clocks are now so accurate.

Experts believe that our bodies act like a watch battery, and that we can stimulate crystals in such a way that they can have this beneficial effect towards our well-being. To put it simply: if we place a crystal close to us, our bodies will tune into the crystal's frequency and vibrations. In effect the crystal will energise and heal us by activating within us our own healing system. Sometimes we just need a little extra help. It's like tuning in to the different channels on a radio; you can tune in for health, energy, peace of mind etc.

Whatever it is we need, there will be a crystal that's said to be able to help. It's just a case of finding the right crystal or crystals.

Healing
I know many say you have to believe in it, and if that means by believing in it, it works, then believe in it. What if there is another explanation? What if it's not the stones or crystals after all, but a belief in them? And if this were true, then the healing mechanism would have to be triggered more from something within, rather than from without. Jesus Christ, the most famous of all healers, often spoke in a coded language before he performed a healing. Here are just a few examples – see if you can spot the code.

"Go! It will be done just as you believed it would," and his servant was healed at that very hour. *Matthew 8 – 13*

Then he touched their eyes and said "According to your faith will it be done to you." *Matthew 9 – 29*

"If you have faith as small as a mustard seed, you can say to this mountain, move from here to there, and it will move. Nothing will be impossible for you." *Matthew 17 – 20*

(Incidentally, I once moved a mountain. I have a friend who introduces me as 'the only man he knows who moved a mountain'. You'll have to read my book 'An Alternative View on Crystal Healing' for the full story) available from Amazon just type in my name for all the details of all my books.

"If you believe, you will receive whatever you ask for in prayer" *Matthew 21 - 22*

"If you can," said Jesus. "Everything is possible for him who believes." Immediately the boy's father explained, "I do believe; help me overcome my unbelief!" *Mark 9 – 23*

"Daughter, your faith has healed you." *Luke 8 – 48*

Hearing this, Jesus said to Jairus, "Don't be afraid; just believe, and she will be healed."
Luke 8 – 50

Are you getting the idea? And no, I'm not getting religious; it's just that if you can understand the code, you can start to understand 'healing'. I am not asking you to abandon your powers of discrimination or personal intuitions in favour of a blind belief. Genuine knowledge and wisdom does not come from gullibility, but it comes from a deep questioning within, until the seeker has genuinely found his or her own answers.

Power, without knowledge, is useless
Do you remember how, in the movie 'Superman', Clark Kent had all the power but not the knowledge? In the early part of the film we see him kicking a football into outer space, and racing a train and winning. His earthly father tells him 'You are here for a reason.' However, this doesn't help Clark Kent to understand why he is different. But when he turns eighteen he takes a green crystal that was sent along as a teaching aid by his real father, Jor-El, and we see him intuitively travel to the frozen north, where he throws the green crystal and sees a crystalline building rise up from the glaciers.

Upon entering the building, Clark finds the green crystal again, and when he places it in the appropriate place on a crystalline control panel, a vision of Jor-El appears and starts to teach him who he is, what he is, where he has come from and why; all about Kryptonian, his home planet, and Kryptonian philosophy. Acquiring all this knowledge takes Clark twelve years, and we next see him no longer an eighteen-year-old boy, but a thirty-year-old man, with all the confidence and knowledge of who he is. We see an amazingly powerful, confident yet graceful take off and fly, and so the real story begins.

Crystal healing
Thought patterns create energy, and it may be that positive thoughts are being amplified with the help of crystals. In truth we still don't know how it works; but for many, it does; so keep an open mind.

A Beginners Guide into Crystal Healing

When I give my talk on the mysteries surrounding gemstones and crystals, I often demonstrate crystal healing, and I must say with some amazing effects. As a Christian I always explain that you wouldn't dream of worshipping aspirin just because it may help with a headache, so I am not for a moment suggesting anybody worships stones. It's just that they didn't have aspirin or chemists years ago and so it was crystals that they used.

In fact there is plenty of evidence to suggest that they used a whole range of crystals to effect cures. These cures using crystal healing techniques have, for many, achieved spectacular successes. How? Going back in time, the priests knew that crystals could bring great benefit to the health of their people. How? Here's one explanation.

Hildegard of Bingen

She was one of the outstanding females of the 12th century and probably of the entire Middle Ages. She was a painter, composer, poet, scientist, playwright, prophet, preacher, abbess – and a healer. Born in 1098, she lived until 1179, an impressive 81 years. From the time she was a young girl, Hildegard had experienced visions. Some of her ideas about gemstones can be traced back to Roman naturalist Pliny and other earlier authors such as Aristotle (4th century B.C.). Many of her directions or recipes involved the preparation of elixirs or the wearing of a stone, especially on the bare skin; soaking the stones in water or wine and then drinking the liquid or pouring it over the troubled spot. Hildegard claimed that angels described to her the healing properties of at least 25 stones. She describes putting an agate (stone) in water when the moon was full and leaving it there for three days and nights, then on the fourth day removing it and using the water for cooking the food for one who was suffering from a certain malady.

Feeling the need to share her visions with the world, at the age of 43 she decided to record what her visions had shown her. Hildegard consulted her confessor, who consulted the Abbot, who consulted the Archbishop of Mainz. Eventually, even the pope was consulted, and all apparently agreed that these were true visions and her knowledge had to come from angels, or at least some sacred source, and was worth recording.

Many of the earliest scholars believed that gemstones and crystals did have strange, often mysterious like powers.

Some personal experiences
The phone rang, "Can I get a piece of Amethyst?" the woman asked. "My friend heard you speak last week and you told her that maybe an Amethyst under her pillow would help her sleep. So she bought one and ever since she's been sleeping like a log." It's nice when you get a call giving positive feedback. The woman went on to tell me that her friend had thought the first night might have been a coincidence – but not the second or third. In fact, two of her friends who had bought Amethysts were both experiencing the same, so she had rung for an Amethyst to help her sleep. Now I sell, all over the world, a 'Themed Power Bracelet' titled 'Sleep Well' which seems to be even more powerful (available on eBay).

A similar call, this time from a man: Could he have another set of healing crystals? He had bought the 'Healer' for his wife, who hadn't enjoyed good health for many years. He couldn't explain it, but she seemed to have got a kind of 'second wind' and was feeling much better than she had for a long time; and she wanted another set for a friend. These days the 'Power Bracelet' the 'Healer' seems to be getting spectacular results if sales are anything to go by.

When I demonstrate crystal healing, I simply pass around a Rose Quartz and Hematite (it's said they work wonders on aches and pains). The audience then can judge for themselves. There is a point when I'll often say, "If anybody's got a headache at this moment in time then you will find it will go," You wouldn't believe the number of people who will come over to me afterwards and say that they hadn't experienced it for themselves, they would never have believed it – but the headache that they had come in with had actually gone.

There was a woman in York (U.K) who had the same story of her headache going, and she decided to buy a special pair of sterling silver eardrops that I make using Rose Quartz and Hematite. She was hoping they might help as she had been suffering for a while from headaches.

Three months later I saw her again in York at another display and she took great delight in showing me that she was still wearing her eardrops. She then said, "You won't believe this, but I haven't had a headache since that day."

A way of connecting

The following information may be of help: find the crystal that best suits you. A full list will follow, clean it – it's called cleansing. Connect with it – that means knowing where it is at all times. Then imagine the desired effect you'd like from it. Then imagine how would you feel if you achieved it – that is, energise it; and then believe. Just as Jesus said: Believe, and it will be yours. You've nothing to lose in trying, but everything to gain. Crystals have a part to play in everyone's lives. Feel free to experiment; but most of all, have fun!

The mystical A to Z of Stones

Be aware that any information given in this book is not intended to be taken as a replacement for medical advice. If in any doubt, always consult a qualified doctor or therapist.

The best way to use the following list is to read the full list of Gemstones and Crystals starting here and at the same time make notes. So, if you are looking for a healing stone for a specific ailment, read the full list, find the stone or stones, and if there are a few, then you might want to narrow them down. There are various ways of narrowing down. Trust your instincts on this one. For instance, you might find, from your research, two gemstone-crystals. It may be that for you, two are ideal. You may be surprised to find that one of the stones is your Birthstone; this would then be the one for you. Or if you have a favourite colour, and if that colour is there on your list, then go with that one. No-one is really sure how all this works; only that, for many, it does. Keep an open mind – many have been pleasantly surprised.

Agate ... The agate probably derives its name from the small river Achates in Sicily, but can be found in many places including Brazil, Madagascar and India. Its rich variations make it a beautiful, multi-faceted stone.

A Beginners Guide into Crystal Healing

Agate cont ...
A powerful healer, it restores body energy and eases stressful situations; gives courage and banishes fear; calms, and increases self-esteem. A stone for good health and fortune, it helps grounding and balance. A stabiliser.

Amazonite .... the 'thinkers' stone. It aids creativity & improves self-worth. A confidence stone. It attracts money and success. A soothing stone; a giver of energy. Solid blue to turquoise, it works on the throat – the fifth Chakra. It inspires hope and is sometimes also called 'the hope stone'.

Amber ... not a stone, but the fossilised resin of extinct pine trees. Good for the throat – the fifth chakra. Worn by actors for good luck and a clear voice. Changes negative energy into positive and is often used as a lucky talisman. It helps the body to heal itself. It is calming, lifting heaviness and allowing happiness to shine through. It prolongs life with a clear mind.

Amethyst ... purple to dark violet, known by a variety of names: Bishop's Stone, Stone of Healing, of Peace, of Love. St. Valentine implied it was one of the best gifts between lovers. Aids creative thinking. Relieves insomnia when placed under the pillow. A powerful aid to spiritual awareness and healing. Helps with meditation, inspiration, intuition and divine love. A stone which helps to attract that special partner.

Apache Tears ... a variant of Obsidian, dark, Smokey, translucent in colour. Good for grounding; transforms; aids in the release of deep emotions. Eases pain, loss and sadness, Neutralises negative magic.

Apatite ... blue in colour. Strengthens muscle tissue, aids co-operation, assists with stuttering and hypertension, and helps to fight viruses. Can help with communications, especially after a misunderstanding.

Aquamarine ... a Beryl, clear blue green. It represents an ocean of love. Preserves innocence, brings spiritual vision, calms the mind and lifts the spirits, releases anxiety and fear. It is recommended for those suffering a lot of grief. Gives insight and perception in dealings with people. Gives protection, often used as a good luck charm. Leads to greater self-knowledge, quickens the mind, and promotes clear and logical thinking.

A Beginners Guide into Crystal Healing

Aventurine ... a variety of quartz, usually green with mica inclusions. Stabilises by inspiring independence, well-being and health. Acts as a general tonic on the physical level. If left in water overnight, it can then be used to bathe the eyes, and similarly to treat skin irritations. Encourages creativity, gives courage, independence, calmness and serenity. It is a money magnet and a good luck stone, a lucky talisman.

Azurite ... deep blue to blue-purple. An aid for meditation, it is used to increase psychic powers as it helps to induce prophetic dreams, intuition and understanding. It's also known as the 'Decision Maker'. With its high copper content it assists the flow of energy throughout the nervous system, strengthens the blood and is used to treat arthritis and joint disabilities.

Beryl ... many colours. The best of the Beryl group are emeralds and aquamarines. In ancient rituals the Beryl was used to bring rain. It is related to the sea and guards its wearer against drowning and sea sickness. Protects against 'mind games'. Helps to stimulate the mind, and increases confidence. In the sixteenth century, it was worn to win arguments and debates.

Bloodstone ... (Heliotrope)... a form of Jasper – dark green in colour, with red flecks. The red flecks are symbolic of Christ's death and his blood spilling onto the stone. Acts on all of the Chakras, a physical healer and a mental balancer. Removes toxins and aligns energies, especially along the spinal cord. Helps prevent miscarriages and eases childbirth. Works to overcome depression and pain of the emotional kind. Calming, grounding and revitalising. A stone to attract wealth, often used in business or legal matters to help attract success.

Calcite ... red, orange, yellow, green and blue (see the Chakras). There is also a clear variety of calcite called Iceland Spar which, when placed over a line on a piece of paper, will produce a double image. Calcite is a strong balancing stone, giving comfort and lifting depression. Also alleviates fear, aids mental clarity, calms turbulent emotions, expands awareness and aids intuition. Good for pancreas and spleen. Clears toxins by gently helping to cleanse the blood.

Carnelian (Cornelian) ... mainly bright orange. The 'friendly one' – it is a very highly evolved healer. A good balancer; can help you connect with your inner self. Good for concentration. Brings joy, sociability and warmth. Good for rheumatism, arthritis, depression, neuralgia, and helps to regularise the menstrual cycle. When coupled with amethyst, purifies consciousness, reverses negative thought and shakes off sluggishness.

A Beginners Guide into Crystal Healing

Cat's Eye ... golden to mid-yellow, green to bluish brown. The Greeks called it 'Cymophane' meaning 'wave-light'. It resembles the contracted pupil of a cat's eye. In the symbolic necklace of 'Vishnu' the green gem was held to represent the earth. A magnetic centre of human passions. It is used to increase beauty and wealth, to protect, and to guard against danger.

Celestite ... white to clear; light blue cluster crystals. Signifies honesty. Helps with tiredness, soothes nerves and stress. Quietens the mind, promotes compassion, expands creative expression, reveals truth.

Chalcedony ... soft blue, translucent, belonging to a large group of crystalline forms and geodes. Stimulates optimism and enhances spiritual creativity. Diminishes nightmares and fear of the dark. A stone that guards travellers, and helps grounding through negative times. Banishes fear, mental illness, hysteria and depression.

Chrysocolla .. blue to blue-green opaque mineral, essentially a copper-element mineral. 'The woman's friend', relieving tension, pains and problems, soothing period pains and pre-menstrual tension. Increases energy, wisdom and peace of mind. Alleviates feelings of guilt, clears all negativity and brings about patience and contentment. Helps to attract love.

Chrysoprase ... an apple-green form of chalcedony, the colour being due to traces of nickel. For wisdom and meditation. Helps the wearer to see clearly into personal problems, especially sexual frustrations and depressions. Worn to lift the emotions, attract friends and shield against negativity.

Citrine ... clear to yellow-orange. Natural Citrine was originally amethyst, transformed by being reheated and burnt in the earth's crust. Helps to clear mental and emotional problems and improve memory. Enhances willpower, optimism and confidence. Helps those who feel they have lost their way in life and need to find a new sense of direction. Strengthens the immune system, improves poor circulation and aids tissue regeneration.

Copper ... mixes easily with other metals; for example, copper, tin and zinc make bronze. Copper is thought to be one of the best transmitters of healing energy. This may be because it has been used very successfully against cholera; it was discovered that men who worked with copper didn't get cholera, and that wearing copper improves the metabolism, reduces inflammation and increases blood flow. Worn next to the skin it soothes arthritis and rheumatism and can kill all kinds of bacteria. Certain bacteria are found in plenty on silver coins but are said never to be found on copper.

A Beginners Guide into Crystal Healing

Coral ... red, pink or white. Calcium calcite was once a living sea creature and is therefore thought to contain 'life essence'. It is used as a protector especially to safeguard children. Sometimes referred to as the 'Tree of Life of the Ocean', it protects and strengthens the wearer's emotional foundation. Also, because it symbolises fertility, it offers a defence against sterility.

Diamond ... a well-known mineral, the purest and hardest substance in nature. It forms the neatest and sharpest of all known cutting edges and is now used in microsurgery with spectacular effect. When used with loving clear intent, it clears blockages and opens the crown Chakra. Amplifies the full spectrum of energies in the mind, body and spirit.

Dioptase ... deep blue to green. Rivals the Emerald in its beauty and holistic healing powers. It empowers the heart with new depth, strength, healthiness, courage, and the ability to love deeply again. Promotes genuine, sincere emotional balance, self-worth and deep well-being; helps heal sadness, heartache, abuse and neglect. A stone for the heart.

Emerald ... green. An excellent general healer, used in ancient times as a blood detoxifier and anti-poison. Improves creativity, imagination, memory and quick-wittedness. Helps the intellect and improves intelligence. Gives power to see the future. Grants success in business ventures and offers patience, harmony, peace and prosperity. An emotional stabiliser.

Fluorite (Fluorspar) ... appears in all rainbow colours. A 'new age' stone that strengthens thought and balances mental energy. Good for meditation. Fluorite clears the mind of stress and aids sleep. Helps physical and mental healing and strengthens bone tissue, especially tooth enamel. Relieves dental disease, viral inflammations and pneumonia.

Garnet ... black, pink-red, yellow-brown, orange or green. A member of a vast gemstone family. A 'knight in shining armour' contains a little of most metals but especially aluminium, silicon and oxygen. A revitalising tonic for the whole body, creating a shield of positive energy; aids in dreams, past lives, self-confidence and personal courage, and attracts love.

Geodes ... are hollow volcanic bubbles containing crystals. All Quartz, Rock Crystal, Amethyst and Opal is formed within geodes. The effect is brought about by the mineral-rich watery fluids percolating into the cavity or hole left by the 'bubble' which occurred in the steaming red hot volcanic lava. Some geodes are huge enough to drive cars through, while others are small enough to fit in the palm of your hand.

Hematite ... a natural ferric oxide, a silver-grey metallic mirror-like stone. You either like or dislike it, there's no 'in between'. To those who like it, it's a very optimistic inspirer of courage and personal magnetism. It lifts gloominess and depression and, when used in conjunction with Carnelian, can prevent fatigue. Good for blood, spleen and generally strengthens the body. Effective during pregnancy; helps with stress.

Jade ... comes in a variety of colours. It's a money magnet, a good luck talisman, and a protector from accidents, evil spirits and bad luck. It encourages long life, safe journeys, wisdom, courage, peace and harmony. The geological term for jade is Nephrite, from the Greek word 'nephros' meaning 'kidney'. As a healer, jade is good for kidneys, bladder, lungs and heart; the immune system, and even high blood pressure.

Jasper ... chalcedony quartz. Multi-coloured. A popular talisman, well liked amongst psychic healers. Protects from all kinds of ailments. It's a powerful healing stone, invigorating and stabilising. It calms troubled minds and helps to slow down the ageing process. Helps those suffering from emotional problems by balancing the physical and emotional needs.

Jet ... a black glass-like substance – fossilised wood, another type of coal, mainly from Whitby in England. Even the jet used in ancient Mesopotamia was thought to have been originally mined in Whitby. Like amber, when rubbed it becomes electrical charged. A good travel aid. Helps increased psychic awareness, guards against witchcraft, demons, melancholy and anxiety, and is very good for manic-depressives.

Kunzite ... pink to dark lilac-rose. Has a high lithium content. Named after Dr. G F Kunz, a noted mineralogist. Good for both the emotional and spiritual heart; reduces depression and mood swings. When held, induces relaxation by releasing tension and stress. A balancer for mind, body, and spirit. Benefits those with any kind of compulsive behaviour.

Kynite ... light blue. Contains aluminium. It is softer lengthways than it is across, and is immune to the forces of other chemicals (such as acids).Brings out our natural ability to manifest things into reality via thoughts and visualisation. Encourages devotion, truth, loyalty and reliability.

Labradorite ...'iridescent feldspar'. Yellow. Pink, green, blue and violet. When in trouble and in doubt, wear a Labradorite. A stone for today, it opens the energy flow to any or all of the Chakra centres, whichever is in greatest need. Brings restful sleep and straightening of the spine.

A Beginners Guide into Crystal Healing

Lapis Lazuli … medium to dark blue with gold pyrite flecks. Called by the ancient Egyptians 'the Stone of Heaven', and thought to be the stone upon which were carved the laws given to Moses. A stone for teachers; helps ease expression and gain higher wisdom and clarity. Good for mental, physical, spiritual, psychic and emotional problems, and well-known for healing the whole. Alleviates fear and eases depression, quiets the mind; helps with creativity, writing, dreams, insight, self-expression and finding inner truth.

Malachite … dark and light bands of green tints. Its name probably comes from the Greek 'malache' ('mallow', as of the colour of green mallow leaf). Egyptians used green Malachite paste for eye make-up. Stimulates physical and psychic vision and concentration. Contains copper and is useful in treating rheumatism and arthritis. Good for raising the spirits, increasing health, hope and happiness. Brings prosperity and is used to guard against all negativity.

Moldavite … formed by a meteorite strike in the Moldau Valley area of the Czech Republic over twelve million years ago. A powerful healing stone, it helps telepathic access to the spiritual laws, and attracts information from higher levels to help us and our earth to become healthier and more spiritual. Helps us to understand our true purpose in life. A stone of transformation.

Moonstone … an opalescent feldspar. In India the Moonstone is a sacred gem, thought to be lucky if given by the groom to his bride. Called the 'Travellers' Stone because it was a favourite protective amulet for those going on perilous journeys. Claimed to promote long life and happiness. It soothes stress and anxiety and is good for period pains and other kindred disorders. A powerful fertility and good luck stone from India.

Mother of Pearl … is the lustrous, opalescent interior of various sea molluscs. Aptly dubbed the 'sea of tranquillity', it creates physical harmony of a gentle but persuasive kind. Calms the nerves. Indicates treasure, chastity, sensitivity and strength. Good for calcified joints and the digestive system. Relaxes and soothes the emotions; helps with sensitivity and stress. Carries the gentle, peaceful healing energy of the sea.

Obsidian Snowflake … not really a stone, but a volcanic glass. Also Obsidian Black, Mahogany and clear. For all those it recognises, it's a powerful healer. Keeps energy well grounded, clears subconscious blocks and brings an insight and understanding of the power behind silence, detachment, wisdom and love. A very lucky talisman, a bringer of good fortune. Was favoured by ancient Mexican cultures to neutralise negative energy and black magic. Good for eyesight, stomach and intestines, and alleviates viral and bacterial inflammations.

Onyx ... black, 'lightweight' Quartz. It can give a sense of courage and help to discover truth. Instils calm and serenity; diminishes depression. Gives self-control whilst aiding detachment and inspiring serenity. A protective stone worn in times of conflict, a student's friend as it encourages concentration and protects against unwise decisions. It is often found in rosaries; it helps to improve devotion, and relieves stress.

Opal ... a silica. The 'Rainbow Stone'. Multi-coloured, it is a wonderful stone to behold, and can be charged with virtually every type of energy needed. It controls temper and calms the nerves. It was sometimes considered unlucky, but (according to Thomas Nichols' book of 1652) this is probably why: *'opalus:- cloudeth the eyes of those that stand about him who wears it, so that they can either not see or not mind what is done before them; for this cause it is asserted to be a safe patron of thieves and thefts.'* Because of its beauty, things were stolen or went missing, hence, according to some, its unlucky label.

Peridot ... clear bright green, also green to yellow (Chrysolite). A good anti-toxin gem, for cleaning most organs and glands. An overall tonic. Used by the Egyptians, Aztecs and Incas to gently help cleanse and heal the physical, including heart, lungs, lymph and muscles. Prized by the Crusaders as 'their' stone. It clears energy pathways, strengthens the 'breath of life' and attracts prosperity, growth and openness. It's also useful for attracting love and opening new doors of opportunity and abundance.

Rhodocrosite ... a solid clear, beautiful pink stone. Good for giving and receiving love. Inspires forgiveness. Heals emotional scars; helps to cope with loneliness, loss, heartache, fears, insecurities and inner child issues. Helps prevent mental breakdown and balances physical and emotional traumas. Soothes and de-stresses the body, cheers the depressed and coaxes back the life force in the very sick.

Rhodonite ... pink with black inclusions. Improves memory, calms the mind and reduces stress. Gives confidence and self-esteem. Cheers the depressed, preserves youth and retards the ageing process. Helps to bring back the life force into the sick. Carries the power to the unobstructed love. Good for emotional trauma, mental breakdown, spleen, kidneys, heart and blood circulation. A very special stone.

A Beginners guide into Crystal Healing

Rock Crystal … also known traditionally as clear Quartz. This stone holds a place of unique importance in the world of gems. It enlarges the aura of everything near to it, by acting as a catalyst to increase the healing powers of other minerals, its vibration resonates with the beat of life, giving Rock Crystal a key role in all holistic practices. Good for the mind and soul, strengthening, cleansing and protecting, especially against negativity.

Rose Quartz … translucent to clear pink. Possesses Healing qualities for the mind. It can help with migraine and headaches. It excites the imagination, helps to release pent-up emotions, lifts spirits and dispels negative thoughts. Eases both emotional and sexual imbalances and increases fertility. Good for spleen, kidneys and circulatory system. Coupled with hematite, works wonders on aches and pains throughout the whole body.

Ruby … blood red. Plays a vital role in micro-surgery as a cauterising instrument. Used to alleviate all kinds of blood disorders, anaemia, poor circulation, heart disease, rheumatism and arthritis. Helps ease worries; lifts the spirits. Improves confidence, intuition and spiritual wisdom, courage and energy; produces joy, dispels fear and strengthens willpower. Gives strength in leadership and success over challengers.

Rutilated Quartz … clear Quartz which contains titanium oxide in the form of slender needles; these amplify the energy of Quartz. It aids healing, eases bronchial problems and increases tissue growth. Also stimulates mental activity and eases depression, improves decisiveness, strength of will, and helps to communicate with the higher self.

Sapphire … related to Ruby. A range of colours, but best known and loved for the dark blue variety. Worn to stimulate the 'third eye', to expand wisdom during meditation. A sacred gem worn by kings to ward off evil. Good for improving the state of mind, increasing clarity of thought and dispelling confusion. Calms the nerves, attracts good influences and strengthens faith. Reputed to lengthen life, keep its wearers looking young. Fortifies the heart and is a guardian of love, feelings and emotions.

Smokey Quartz … looks exactly as its name implies – Smokey. A grounding stone . Ideal around electrical goods such as computers, because it disperses negative patterns and vibrations. It can draw out and absorb negative energies, replacing them with positive. Alleviates moods, depression and other negative emotions; protects against despair, grief and anger. Used in meditation, it helps explore the inner self by penetrating dark areas with light and love. A 'Dream Stone'

Sodalite … deep blue with veined white flecks; often mistaken for Lapis Lazuli, but lacks the golden flecks. Calms and clears the mind, enhancing communication and insight with the higher self. A good stone for people who are over-sensitive and defensive. Brings joy and relieves a heavy heart. When placed at the side of the bed it can make a sad person wake up full of the joys of spring. Imparts youth and freshness to its wearer. When coupled with Rhodonite it produces the 'Elixir of Life'. (For more information see my book 'Gemstones and Crystal Elixirs' available from Amazon Kindle).

Tiger Eye … generally associated with yellow to chocolate-brown. An iridescent combination of colour, resembling the gleaming eye of a tiger at night. The stone has a shifting lustre of golden light across it. It Inspires brave but sensible behaviour with great insight and clearer perception. Fights hypochondria and psychosomatic diseases. A true 'confidence stone'. It attracts good luck, protects from witchcraft, and is an ideal 'worry stone' (let the stone do the worrying). Always carry one for protection.

Topaz … many different colours, the most popular being rose-red to pure white. Named after the island Topazion. Known as the 'abundant one'; a stone of strength; a charm against fires and accidents. Promotes good health by overcoming stress, depression, exhaustion, fears and worries. Good for soothing, tranquillising, calming and protecting.

Tourmaline … has a colour for all seven of the Chakras. A master physician from the mineral world, working on all Chakra levels. A strong protector against misfortune and misunderstandings, it attracts goodwill, love and friendships. It settles troubled minds, gives confidence, inspires, calms the nerves, expands mental energy and helps clarity of thought.

Turquoise … an opaque, light blue to green mineral. A sacred stone to native American Indians, and a powerful talisman to the Egyptians and the Turkish. A lucky stone, a protector against radiation and dark forces: a talisman favoured by horse-riders. A good all-round general healer, gentle, cooling and soothing; a stone that brings wisdom and psychic connection to the Universal Spirit. Turquoise strengthens and aligns all Chakras and energy fields. An absorber of negativity, a guardian against failure and poverty.

Unikite … usually green with red patches. A variety of granite. Its name is taken from the Unaka range of mountains in North Carolina, USA. Autumnal in colour, it is a beautiful stone. It helps the wearer to relax and find peace of mind. It works mainly on a higher plain than the physical, going beyond into the spiritual world to find truth, bring an understanding the true cause of disease and discomfort.

Zircon ... from the Arabic word 'Zarkun' ('vermilion'). Similar to Diamond in lustre and colour and often used as a substitute for diamonds. Known as the 'stone of virtue', it strengthens the mind and brings joy to the heart. Represents vitality, and works with the 'crown' Chakra, helping to connect to Universal Truth. Good for intuition, integrity, insomnia and depression.

Colour – and the Chakras

Another useful guide when choosing crystals could be their colour. In Sanskrit there are original teachings about an energy system known as the 'Chakras'. When seen clairvoyantly, Chakras are wheels of light and colour. There are seven of them. The first one is found at the base or root – that is, around the base of the spine. The second is the sacral or spleen, the third is the solar plexus, and the fourth is the heart. The fifth is the throat, the sixth is the brow or 'third eye', and the seventh and final one is the crown. It's said we need all these energy centres to be open so as to enjoy optimum health. Each is associated with a colour, and these colours are the seven colours of the rainbow, and are in the same running order.

Each Chakra is linked with a particular colour in the spectrum of light. The 'root' Chakra is red; the 'sacral' or 'spleen' Chakra is orange; the 'solar plexus' Chakra is yellow; the 'heart' Chakra is green; the 'throat' Chakra is blue; the 'brow' chakra is indigo; and finally the 'crown' Chakra is violet. I know it all may sound like gobbledygook, but the human body requires light to maintain itself. For example, our bodies produce vitamin D – necessary to make our bones and teeth strong and healthy – and this is increased as a result of exposure to sunlight. Think about this: where does the vitamin D come from? One minute it's not there and the next it is. What makes the difference? Stepping out into sunlight does – so light has a power, and you can use this knowledge to your benefit when choosing the right gemstone or crystals.

Birthstones

Next you will find my list of twelve birthstones. In my research I studied over seventeen different lists. My list is the same as the Bible's list for Aries, Virgo and Pisces. These lists have been heavily researched. However, I believe my list to be authentic, and in my book 'An Alternative View on Crystal Healing' I explain how I found my list.

A Beginners guide into Crystal Healing

The second list gives the most popular Precious stones for the United Kingdom; and the third list is taken from the Bible; a New Jerusalem'.

BIRTHSTONES

Zodiac Star signs	*My list* Semi-precious Stones	Precious Stones	Bible Rev. 21-19
ARIES (21 Mar - 20 Apr)	Red Jasper	Diamond	Jasper
TAURUS (21 Apr – 21 May)	Rose Quartz	Emerald	Sapphire
GEMINI (22 May – 21 Jun)	Black Onyx	Pearl	Chalcedony
CANCER (22 June – 22 Jul)	Mother of Pearl	Ruby	Emerald
LEO (23 Jul – 23 Aug)	Tiger Eye	Peridot	Sardonyx
VIRGO (24 Aug – 22 Sep)	Carnelian	Sapphire	Carnelian
LIBRA (23 Sep – 23 Oct)	Green Aventurine	Opal	Chroysolite
SCORPIO (24 Oct – 22 Nov)	Rhodonite	Topaz	Beryl
SAGITTARIUS (23 Nov – 21 Dec)	Sodalite	Turquoise	Topaz
CAPRICORN (22 Dec – 20 Jan)	Obsidian Snowflake	Garnet	Chrysoprase
AQUARIUS (21 Jan – 19 Feb)	Blue Agate	Amethyst	Jacinth
PISCES (20 Feb – 20 Mar)	Amethyst	Aquamarine	Amethyst

A Beginners Guide into Crystal Healing

Discovering the 'true' Birthstones.
I discovered that different continents favoured their own 'home-grown' gemstones and crystals, and that it was only a few hundred years ago that people first discovered how to cut a diamond (it takes a diamond to cut a diamond). Astrology is over six thousand years old, which means that a diamond couldn't have been an original birthstone. In the end, because of all these different lists, I decided the only way would be to take the mean average. That is: if the majority of my differing sources said Red Jasper was the birthstone for Aries then that was good enough for me; and so this was how I got my list- by using the mean average.

Imagine: I now had a list of twelve stones – but was it the right list? How could you find out? I asked well over two thousand people to help with my research, to see if I had got it right (if anyone can get it right!). To test my list I decided to put all the birthstones, in the form of tumblestones, into a basket. Then I passed the basket around, at the same time asking everyone if they would select a stone that they liked. I also asked them to tell me their star signs. Surprisingly, as it turned out, sometimes as many as 70% seemed to pick out their own stones, but the bigger surprise was that those who didn't pick out their own birthstone, many picked out their 'opposite'. That means for example, if they were Aries, then instead of picking out Red Jasper (their own birthstone) they picked out Green Aventurine, their 'opposite' stone (Libra).

A secret code
During my research I came across the 'Law of Polarity'. This states that everything has an opposite – for example: night and day, hot and cold, right and wrong, Ying and Yang etc. In astrology it means the opposite star sign becomes very important. That is, *the meaning of one is enhanced by the knowledge of the other.* If you do read you're your horoscopes, why not in future, for fun, read both your own and your opposite star sign. It may help you to gain a fuller picture.

If you imagine your own star sign as representing you – the 'you' others can see – then your opposite is representative of your inner world, a world others can't see. A world from within: your inner thoughts: a world only you can visit. Finally as we go through mid-life we 'flip' over to the other opposite side. It's called 'The Law of Polarity'

A Beginners Guide into Crystal Healing

A list of 'opposites'

Aries	opposite star sign	Libra
Taurus		Scorpio
Gemini		Sagittarius
Cancer		Capricorn
Leo		Aquarius
Virgo		Pisces
Libra		Aries
Scorpio		Taurus
Sagittarius		Gemini
Capricorn		Cancer
Aquarius		Leo
Pisces		Virgo

I designed and produced a beautiful range of bookmarks around this information. My bookmarks are available now on eBay; just use my I.D code to find my shop **rwwdhp2009** which is on eBay.co.uk. Regarding my book 'Astrology the Secret Code' (available on Kindle - Amazon). I was delighted when I received this testimonial from Mary:-

Dear Robert,
Thank you for the research that you have done to produce a great little book (Astrology the Secret Code) which has helped to settle many arguments. I am a religious education teacher in a catholic school, a practising Catholic with a degree in history and philosophy. I have been made to feel guilty about my interest in Astrology and Crystals because of my faith, but you have given me some fantastic tools to argue my corner. Mary UK

Sometimes books can just seem to speak to you and just when it's needed, so it's always nice to receive letters saying just that: - *Robert,*
I want to say how fantastic I think your books are and I have read them several times since reading them initially. One particular poignant part I'd like to point out: I found when I read in the last paragraph of the 'Change your Life' book I realised just much you really had indeed understood me and my need for direction and truly have allowed me the confidence and strength to know and believe I can achieve whatever I want in life. So I want to thank you from the bottom of my heart – you are an inspiration. Sandra UK

A Beginners Guide into Crystal Healing

During my research, I was given the opportunity to read a book that had been printed in 1652. This book was so old that the pages had to be opened very carefully so as not to damage either the fragile paper or its outer leather cover.

The book turned out to be fascinating. I had the chance to read the original 'Old English Text' about the Magical, Mysterious, and Healing properties of gems and Crystals.

A LAPIDARY or THE HISTORY OF PRETIOUS STONES

With cautions for the undeceiving of all those that deal with Pretious

Thomas Nicols

Sometimes of Jesus College in Cambridge

Printed by Thomas Buck. Printer to the Universitie
1652

Thomas Nicols was a learned man, a scholar and a translator; but couldn't understand how is fellow scholars could believe that various precious stones had supernatural mystical powers, so the explained to him their views of stories of stones changing colour for their owners as a way of showing that danger was near. The Loadstone being magnetic had strange invisible effects on iron fillings; we know them to day as magnets and compasses.

However Thomas Nicols being a committed Christian saw these stories in very simple terms of Black or White. That is, to him, it was either God's work and therefore it was OK, being 'Divine' or it was the devil's work and therefore satanic and diabolic and to be avoided.

So it was in 1652 at Jesus College, Cambridge that Thomas Nicols produced his book on Lapidary, a guide to Gemstones and their mysterious powers.

It was only 200 years earlier that the first printing press had been produced and 100 years since Copernicus had published his treatise; that the sun is a star and that all the planets revolved around it and the earth is simply one of them. Isaac Newton was only 10 years of age and would 35 years later, from the same College, publish his theory of 'Universal Gravitation'.

So it was a credit to Thomas Nicols that he reported so faithfully the thinking of his time whilst still having so many personal doubts of his own. Nearly 350 years later, modern man can now explain many things that earlier man could not. Thomas Nicols did not know for example about the 'Placebo Effect' or the 'Power of suggestion'; the electrical field found within man or the vibrating frequency within the Crystals, or even the Earth's Magnetic Field. If he had known, then he would not have been so troubled about what his fellow scholars were saying.

Enjoy reading some of the extracts from his book, faithfully reproduced unabridged.

Thomas Nicols 1652

"Surely, we live not in the most unknowing times of the World, nay, never was this part of the World fuller knowledge than now, it is wherein many are blest with excellent gifts and endowments by which they are enabled to enquire more thoroughly into its natures and causes of things"

Adults Section !!!

Diamond ... "If a true Diamond be put upon the head of a woman without her knowledge, it will make her in her sleep if she be faithful to her husband, to cast herself into his embraces, but if she be an adulteress, to turn away from him".

Amethyst ... "Arstotle saith of it, that it being applied to the navel, or worn about the navel, it will hinder the ascension of vapours; the reason, it draweth the vapours to its self and doth disguise them. It sharpeneth the wit, diminisheth sleep. Good for resisting of poison".

A Beginners Guide into Crystal Healing

Saphire ... "If it be worn by an adulterer, by loosing its splendour it will discover his adultery and that the wearing of it, both hinder the erections that are caused by Venus. Lustful thoughts or wicked spirit are the causes of such undue erections of the flesh ... keepeth men chaste and therefore is worn of Priests".

Agate ... "strange things of the virtue of this stone as it doth excite passions, move melancholy, doth hinder the fits of the epileptic".

'Power Gems'
Over the years I have been continually asked for various 'Healing Gifts' that would be suitable to give to loved ones, family and friends. So the idea of 'Themed' power Gems was born. It's curious how a business can grow; but once the idea was accepted it was then that the next idea came, and that was, 'Why not use combinations of stones' and then the various titles just seemed to arrive. Using the knowledge gained after all the research; I came up with the 'Power Gem' range of gifts.

With titles such as:- 'To Remove Aches and Pains', 'The healer', 'Fertility', 'Good Luck', 'Peace of Mind', 'For Willpower', 'Imagine', 'Energy Booster', 'To Lift depression', 'Elixir of Life', and 'Adults Only', you get the idea.

With this range my audiences could decide for themselves which 'Power Gem' would suit them most. Very quickly I discovered just how popular these were and surprisingly just how effective they were. People were not just buying them for themselves but for their family and friends. It was then that I decided to help further by writing a Mini-Guide to accompany each gift and as people wanted to know more, that was when I decided to go into writing books as well as giving talks. Before I reproduce some extracts from this Mini-Guide for you to read, I would like to relate some very interesting, and yet typical, stories.

I was giving a talk and demonstration at a local home for the retired, a sheltered home. When I had finished, the warden, a women in her mid-thirties, asked if I could make her a special gift for her mother, whose birthday was just a week away. She had had an idea for a gift, something a little unusual and special.

A Beginners Guide into Crystal Healing

She asked me if it would be possible, by using my knowledge, to produce a Gift which would be suitable, with the title of 'Peace of Mind'. It was because every year when she asked her mum what she would like for her birthday her mum always replied "Just give me Peace of Mind, that's all I ask, just give me 'Peace of Mind' and that year, she did. By using Green Aventurine, Rose Quartz and Rhodonite, I was able to present the warden with her new gift, one which is now a firm favourite.

A week later I was giving a talk at a Catholic Church in Bradford (UK), where I told them this little story. Not surprisingly on that night I completely sold out and even finished up having to take orders.

At another sheltered home in Oldham (UK), many of the ladies were buying the 'Adults Only', I think as a joke. One told me that it was for daughter as a little wedding gift, it was only for a bit of fun, and she knew that her daughter would find it amusing.

One of the care workers at the home asked if I did 'party plan', because she thought a lot of her friends and neighbours would be interested if she could hold a party. So we made a firm date and then duly turned up on the night. One of the ladies from the sheltered home was there and she was continually warning her friends to be careful of the 'Adults Only' because, she said, "they don't half work". Only modesty stopped me from asking exactly what she meant; she looked the sort that would have told me. Because of her testament that night, you won't be surprised but I completely sold out.

Extracts from the Mini-Guide
Power gems are a unique group of Gemstones and Crystals that have been carefully linked in harmony to unite their individual mystic powers and provide a Holistic Force which can help revive Health, increase Wealth, bring Peace and provide Energy.

If just one Crystal or Gemstone does possess power and does have a potency, then just imagine how exciting the prospect of having three Crystals and Gemstones linked together.

A Beginners Guide into Crystal Healing

The thought of such power from each stone being united with the powers of the others and amplified can be awesome. Most of my Power Gems contain three Gemstones or Crystals, a powerful number in itself, being representative of Mother Earth as well as the Holy Trinity.

The Healer

I have united the three most powerful Healing Gemstones and Crystals, and now you can read why ….

Carnelian - The friendly one. It is a very evolved healer, mentioned many times in both the Old and New Testaments of the bible.

Red Jasper - Well known as a powerful healing stone and a provider of strength. Mentioned in the New Testament in Revelations 21:19 – "The first foundations of the walls of the New Jerusalem were made of Jasper". Represents, Aries in Astrology, the first energy of the life cycle – "On the first day of spring, a commencement force of purest energy revitalizes the Earth".

Rock Crystal - This stone holds a place of unique importance in the world of Gems. It enlarges the aura of everything near to it and acts as a catalyst to increase the healing powers of other minerals. Co-ordinates all holistic practices.

Good Luck

These three powerful Gemstones are well known for their Good Fortune.

Obsidian Snowflake - Favoured by ancient Mexican cultures, to neutralise negative magic, a very lucky talisman, a bringer of good fortune.

Green Aventurine – Green is a colour associated with God and in Astrology linked with Libra. Libra is a cardinal Air sign of the Zodiac and Air is the Breath of Life. Libra is also the seventh sign of the Zodiac, which is also favoured as God's number. Green Aventurine was favoured by Carl Faberge, the Russian craftsman famous for 'Faberge Eggs'.

Moonstone – In India, Moonstone is a sacred Gemstone and is given to the bride by the groom on their wedding day, as a token of Good Luck and Fortune. The moon has the most influence and power of all the heavenly bodies over our Earth.

Peace of Mind

A combination of stones to bring peace, harmony and tranquillity into your surroundings; to capture the stillness in movement.

Green Aventurine – Green is said to be God's colour. A stone well known for easing anxiety and fears. A talisman, a bringer of good fortune.

Rose Quartz – A love stone, which also helps to relieve migraine and headaches. Releases pent up emotions, high spirits and dispels negative thoughts.

Rhodonite – Improves memory, calms the mind, reduces stress, gives confidence and self-esteem. Cheers the depressed, preserves youth and retards the ageing process, a very special stone.

For Willpower

The most powerful combination of Gems and Crystal which can be used to boost willpower e.g. to lose weight or stop smoking.

Rose Quartz – Healing qualities for the mind, helps to release pent up emotions whilst dispelling negative thoughts.

Black Onyx – It can give a sense of courage and helps to discover truth. Gives self-control, whilst aiding detachment. Helps relieve stress.

Rock Crystal – This stone holds a place of unique importance in the world of gems. It enlarges the Aura of everything near to it and acts as a catalyst to increase the healing powers of other minerals. Co-ordinates all holistic practices.

Adults Only

These powerful stones combine to create the most imaginative aphrodisiac. A very sensuous combination.

Rose Quartz – Well known as a love stone with a beautiful colour of pink.

Amethyst – A romantic stone, very helpful for meditation, inspiration and divine love.

Carnelian – A stone on the breastplate of King Solomon. This power stone represents passion and energy and like Amethyst, Carnelian contains iron traces which give its seductive colour. A solid dependable stone.

A Beginners Guide into Crystal Healing

To remove Aches and Pains

Three gemstones designed for easing aches and pains.

Rose Quartz – Rose Quartz is made up of minute crystals with traces of Titanium, a metal element, which gives it profound strength.

Hematite – There are many ailments which benefit from a source of iron. When united with Rose Quartz, this steel-like stone works wonders with aching bones and bruised skin.

Rock Crystal – Once again the Rock Crystal acts as a catalyst to increase the active powers within Rose quartz and Hematite.

To Lift Depression

Three powerful gemstones, which bring joy and happiness and help to remove sadness.

Carnelian – The friendly one, Carnelian is a highly evolved healing stone. Providing good concentration. Brings joy, sociability and warmth.

Hematite – To those who like it, it can be a very optimistic inspirer of courage and personal magnetism. Lifts gloominess and depression.

Tiger Eye – Inspires brave, sensible behaviour. The confidence stone, fights hypochondria and psychosomatic diseases.

Elixir of Life

To produce an Elixir, we should first wash the Gemstones. Then place them in a glass of clear water and leave them overnight, ideally in the light of a full moon. The Elixir of Life should be sipped slowly in a ritualistic manner. This is a powerful approach, which appeals ideally to the imagination.

Rhodonite – Preserves youth and retards the aging process. Helps to bring back the life force in the sick, carries the power to the unobstructed love. A very special stone.

Sodalite – Brings joy and relieves a heavy heart. Imparts youth and freshness to its wearer. (When combined with Rhodonite, can produce the Elixir of Life).

Imagine

We use the lovely title from John Lennon's song "Imagine", as these stones really are designed for a very special purpose. Power beyond imagination holds the key to all changes of life. The fine tints of these stones are designed to help us reach a level within the mind, where all things become possible.

Imagine cont ....

Rose Quartz – Helps to excite the imagination, helps to relieve pent up emotion. Lifts spirits and dispels negative thoughts.

Amethyst – Aids creative thinking. A very special and powerful aid to spiritual awareness. Very helpful for meditation, inspiration and intuition.

Green Aventurine – Green is said to be God's colour. Stabilising through inspiring independence. A stone to encourage a higher level of meditation.

Energy Booster

A combination of three gemstones to boost energy.

Carnelian – Good for shaking off sluggishness and helps us become more vigorous and alert. A gemstone used on the breastplate of King Solomon, maybe to boost his energy, perhaps because he was known to have had 1,000 wives. Carnelian is associated with Virgo, the sixth sign of the Zodiac and the element Earth.

Amethyst – When coupled with Carnelian, Amethyst becomes a very powerful energy booster. Amethyst is tinted by irradiated iron and iron is one of the six active body minerals essential for life. It strengthens muscles, enriches the blood and increases resistance to illness.

Rock Crystal – Has the power to enlarge the aura of other Gemstones and in this case it increases power to store energy. In Greek mythology, Rock Crystal was known as Holy Water frozen by the Gods of Olympus.

An Observation

For many years I have researched, studied and even demonstrated crystal healing in front of well over one hundred thousand people. I have read books, reports and articles. I have used and searched the Internet. I have seen and heard so many stories about healing crystals. In fact I have served my apprenticeship 'out in the field', so to speak, in front hundreds of groups representing lots of organisations, with people coming from all walks of life. So what are we to make of all this information? Is it real, or could we take it all with a pinch of salt and ignore it? I think it's not whether crystals work, but how do they work?

One of my observations over the years has got to be that men are more cynical than women.

A Beginners Guide into Crystal Healing

However, there is a kind of hush that settles down over the men once I am into my presentation. I think it's because the men are surprised to hear, in words, what women seem to already know; and it's something women seem to have a feel for intuitively. Women seem to accept crystal healing quite easily. On the other hand, academics find it very difficult, if not almost impossible, to accept a simple, esoteric, new-age philosophy. Many books written by academics seem to find it difficult to comprehend the simplistic, holistic approach to healing with crystals. My point is this: in the end you will have to make up your own mind. I suggest you keep an open mind.

Can't see the obvious?
Here's a little story to make my point:
Sherlock Holmes and Dr. Watson go camping. During the night, Holmes wakes his friend. "Watson, look up at the sky and tell me, what do you see?" And Watson says:" I see a million stars." Holmes asks, "What does that tell you?" The good doctor thinks about it and says; "Theologically, I can see that God is all powerful. Astronomically, it tells me there are a million galaxies. Astrologically, I observe that Saturn is in Leo. Meteorologically, I suspect tomorrow will be a beautiful day. Horologically, I deduce that it is 2.30 am. What does it tell you Holmes?" "Watson, my dear friend," said the great detective, "it tells me someone has stolen our tent"

Ask an academic if he or she believes in God, and here you will find your first problem: when they ask you to define what you mean by the word 'God'. You'll move into a world of semantics and miss the importance of a simple understanding. It doesn't get any easier when you understand that there is more than one truth. For example, you could ask one person to take a ride on a big dipper at the fun fair, and another to watch. Then see if they can both describe 'a big dipper' to someone else who doesn't have a clue as to what one is. Although they would be describing the same ride, they will give two different versions. It wouldn't even matter if you put them both onto ride at the same time; you will still get two different versions. Over the years I have come across many people who are walking around, who will swear blind that a crystal or crystal healer cured them of whatever problems, illness or troubles they had.

A Beginners Guide into Crystal Healing

So whilst many are in denial, the rest are witnessing miracles that sometimes just beggar belief.

Here's food for thought: today is a gift; that's why it's called the present.

'Power for Life – Power Bracelets'

After Power Gems came our special 'Themed Power Bracelets', but do remember that any information given in this book is not intended to be taken as a replacement for medical advice. If in any doubt, always consult a qualified doctor or therapist.

Imagine if you could feel the Power; to rediscover the Zest, the Energy and the Buzz and start enjoying life again, life's not a rehearsal.

Our Power bracelets have evolved over many years and have gained a lot of their inspiration from the power beads worn by, for example, the Dalai Lama; and also the rosary beads used for devotion in many churches including the Catholic Church. Buddhist would know them more by the name 'Mala' (ma-la) from a ancient Sanskrit language roughly meaning when translated 'Rose or Garland'.

Here to help you further, with your understanding of Crystal Healing. Imagine if each 'Power for Life' power bracelet contained within it a kind of "Inner-Technology" a memory and that this "Technology" once activated, this power is guaranteed to help attract abundance in every area of life, from careers to relationships, from changing luck to miraculous healings. Once discovered it can naturally activate a kind of mental calm that comes from a great feeling of peace and tranquillity. It helps to trigger the body's own healing mechanism, and then it can easily start to attract more love, health, wealth and creativity, it can improve opportunities and bring with it a wisdom well beyond any of our current understanding.

This "Inner-Technology" amazingly seems to contain a knowledge of the true essence of life, it's a little like having the very latest 'Pentium Chip' in your computer however this chip, this "Inner-Technology" this supernatural help line seems to be thousands of years in advance of anything we yet know of today and yet, and here is a paradox, it must have actually been around from the beginning of time; be amazed and discover how it can work for you.

A Beginners guide into crystal Healing

With every 'Themed Power Bracelet' we always include a free guide book, 'How to Activate the Hidden Power in Gemstones and Crystals'. Why not check out my latest book (130 pages) 'An Alternative View on Crystal Healing' and is now available on both eBay and Amazon Kindle. It's based on an idea of; what if it's not the crystal but the belief in the crystal. It wouldn't make any difference to the outcome, but the knowledge of knowing the difference could.

Here is a useful extract from my book:- BK9 'Lucky Gemstone and Crystal Talisman, Charms and Amulets'.

Luck:-
Although there's no basis in science for luck and maybe luck is only an illusion of control, but control is what we try to seek in a random world. Themed 'Power Bracelets' can give the owner a sense of preparedness, a feeling of control and encourage a more positive outlook on life, which in itself may give us that 'edge', an extra push to help improve our life, and change if for the better.

Our journey through life is all about personal empowerment and the freedom of choice, and what we can do with it. Be prepared, with the help of our 'Themed Power Bracelets', Gemstones and Crystals don't be surprised when positive changes start to come.

After Power Gems came our 'Themed Power Bracelets, and these now sell all over the world. If you, like me, enjoy making gemstone and crystal gifts; then the following list may be useful.

Dream Maker … *Turn your deepest dreams into reality, achieve your goals, your life's ambition and realise your true destiny …*
Red Jasper, Green Aventurine, Amethyst and Hematite.

To Remove Aches and Pains … *Stones selected for easing aches and pains. An ancient healing treatment …*
Red Jasper, Rock Crystal, Rose Quartz and Hematite

Fertility …Sometimes nature may need a helping hand, allow these gemstones and crystals to help increase your fertility …
Rock Crystal, Rose Quartz, Moonstone and Hematite

The Healer … Attract your share of good health, restore your balance and harmony, regenerate and bring back wholeness …
Carnelian, Rock Crystal, Red Jasper and Hematite

Allergy-Free … Are you unusually sensitive to normally harmless substances? Then try this natural way to eliminate your allergy's …
Tiger Eye, Green Aventurine, Red Jasper and Hematite

Stress–Buster … Relax, 'just switch on' your power bracelet and become calm and stress-free. It takes only seconds let your Power Bracelet take the strain ….
Rose Quartz, Amethyst, Mother of Pearl and Hematite

Vitality … Regain and experience more energy, vitality and strength. Use nature's own energy 'boosters' …
Carnelian, Amethyst, rock Crystal and Hematite.

Sleep Well … Enjoy a good nights rest, a deep sleep with sweet dreams, feel refreshed and then awakened anew …
Amethyst, Rock Crystal, Rose Quartz and Hematite

Friendship … Given or received with love and affection, a bracelet symbolizing the sign of true friendship …
Carnelian, Rhodonite, Rose Quartz and Hematite

A Beginners Guide into Crystal Healing

Tranquillity ... Gain 'Peace of Mind', relax and reflect away all your worries by harmonizing with nature ...
Green Aventurine, Rhodonite, Rose Quartz and Hematite

Travel Safe ... The 'St. Christopher' of gemstones for safe journeys. To always travel in style and arrive safely ...
Obsidian Snowflake, Mother of Pearl, Tiger Eye and Hematite

Lose a Stone ... A must for the weight-watcher, helps to 'boost' you willpower to loose weight and also helps stop smoking ...
Black Onyx, Rock Crystal, Rose Quartz and Hematite

For True Love ... Open the flood gates to love and romance, help find your soul-mate and achieve perfect harmony ...
Amethyst, Rhodonite, Rose Quartz and Hematite

Good Luck ... Attract your share of good fortune, help find success and achieve prosperity ...
Green Aventurine, Moonstone, Obsidian Snowflake and Hematite

Happiness ... Attract joy and happiness by removing sadness and having it replaced with pleasure ...
Sodalite, Carnelian, Rose Quartz and Hematite

Gemstone-Crystal Rituals

Once we have found our gemstones or crystals – and some say it may be more a matter of the stones finding us, rather than us them – there are one or two practical rituals that we should perform. The first is to cleanse it. This isn't a bad idea when you consider the number of people who may have touched or handled it. There is a school of thought that says stones can hold negative energy or imbalances and that cleansing or washing removes this, wiping them clean so as to restore them to their original clarity. Some go as far as to suggest that cleansing should be done every time the stones have been used for healing.

There are many ways of cleansing. You could just simply hold the stone under the tap and then dry it. You could hold it under running water for a few minutes and then place it in the sun to dry out. Placing stones onto a large crystal cluster will clean and energies them.

You could hold the crystal in the smoke of an incense or smudge stick. Herbs and spices such as sandalwood, cedar, sage and frankincense are used for their purifying qualities. The vibrations of pure sound can energetically clean a stone; a bell, gong or tuning fork can be used for this purpose. You could take a deep breath and blow over the crystal whilst imagining that you are clearing away negativities. You could even bury the stone in the ground for twenty-four hours and let Mother Nature re-charge the crystal.

Connecting
After the cleansing rituals you need to connect with the stone or crystal. How do you know if you are connected? If someone asks where your crystal or gemstone is and you don't know, then you are not connected; but if you do know where it is, then you are connected. If you lost the stone and didn't know, then you were not connected. To be connected you have to know where it is at any time, day or night.

Aladdin and his Lamp
Remember the story of Aladdin and his three wishes? In the story, you'll remember, the Genie in the lamp was obliged to give three wishes to whoever owned the lamp; it didn't matter to the Genie who made the wishes. So before Aladdin could get his three wishes, firstly he had to own the lamp, and secondly he had to have rubbed it. Here's the point: do you think if, in real life, you had Aladdin's lamp, there would ever be a time when you wouldn't know where it was? It's the same with your crystal. If at any time you are asked where it is and you don't know, then you are connected.

Connecting
That's why some will put their crystal under their pillow and sleep on it. The ritual part would be if they consciously touched the stone just before they went to sleep. If they could do this again first thing in the morning, whilst coming out of sleep and before getting out of bed, then they would be connected.

Another ritual could be to have the stone in the lounge, and at the same time each day 'visit' the stone and touch it, or turn the stone three times, like winding up a clock. You could do this three times a day.

A Beginners Guide into Crystal Healing

In fact, the more ritualistic, the more connected. It's no coincidence that churches are full of rituals, why? Because rituals can help us to connect. Why do we want to connect? So we can experience the benefits of being connected.

Interesting feedback
Over many years I have received many letters, phone calls and e-mails, all relating to how a gemstone or crystal has helped in one way or another. I know some will say, "It's all in the mind," and others will say, "You have to believe in it," whilst others still will say, "It's mind over matter," and many more might say, "It's all nonsense." Whatever their viewpoint most people are willing to give gemstones and crystals a try. I suggest you keep an open mind.

In my book 'An Alternative view on Crystal Healing', you will find a story of how I was told, after five days of meditation at an 'inner child' workshop that my life's mission was to 'de-mystify the mysteries'. Isn't life strange? Look at what I now do: I give talks and workshops on the mysteries surrounding gemstones-crystals, and I write on the subject.

During my talks and displays on the mysteries that surround gemstones and crystals, I explain that there is a formula – 'When imagination and willpower are in conflict, then imagination will always win', its set in granite. Take my word for it: it works. Once you are able to grasp the meaning, it can change your life for ever. Willpower will not force a crystal to work, but imagination can. You have a power beyond the imagination. Learn how to use it; and let the 'magic' of life begin.

In hypnosis, if you give a person a glass of water and instruct them to "take a sip", then tell them they have just taken a truth serum and ask them a question, they will be compelled to tell the truth, irrespective of the consequences.

Imagine telling a person so shy that they have drunk a new drug that's just come onto the market and causes everyone who takes it to just ooze an amazing confidence, becoming so attractive to the opposite sex that they attract admirers like a magnet. There's little doubt that this person would fail. Or you could tell them they are so confident they can't possibly fail their exams, or driving test ...

A Beginners Guide into Crystal Healing

The processes governing our subconscious mind, the power behind our imagination, our physical and emotional well-being, are all deeply rooted and nourished from the source of Life itself. The ability to contact this deeper source of life comes from within. So with the help of Gemstones and Crystals enjoy your journey, a journey of discovery.

Whatever has happened in your life up until now, whatever you may have dreamed of, believed in or hoped for, remember it's all now in the past and can't be changed, however hard you wish it could. A new life, a new chance and a new hope now awaits you. But you yourself must take the first step and do the reaching. What was it that Spock used to say? – "Live long and prosper"

Use your Wisdom – the ability to think and act utilising your knowledge, experience, understanding, common sense and insight. We are part of creation, just as gemstones and crystals are. We are all connected to the universe; by looking beyond our world we will in time realise that the things which we seek outside, we already have within.

Gemstones and Crystals are tools to help to connect to that which we desire. It's like making a phone call to a helpline: the Gemstones and Crystals are the phone, we do the dialling and the asking, and then we hope that the Universal Life Force can help.

Glossary of Healing Stones
The following information is not authoritative, but a fluid interpretation drawn from many sources. It is always advisable to consult your own Doctor before embarking on any course of self-treatment or using any type of alternative therapy. On no account should a Gemstone or Crystal ever be swallowed.

A
Aches & Pains (easing of)	Rose Quartz, Rock Crystal & Hematite
Abdominal Colic	Mother of Pearl & Obsidian Snowflake
Accidents (prevention of)	Yellow Carnelian & Tiger Eye
Addiction	Amethyst & Black Onyx
Adults Only (aphrodisiac)	Rose Quartz, Amethyst & Carnelian
Acidity	Green Jasper & Rock Crystal

A Beginners Guide into Crystal Healing

Ageing (to retard general Process of)	'Elixir of Life' Sodalite & Rhodonite
Aggression (moderation of)	Carnelian & Amethyst
Alcoholism	Amethyst & Black onyx
Allergies	Red Jasper, Rock Crystal & Carnelian
Anaemia	Citrine & Hematite
Anger	Carnelian & Amethyst
Angina	Rose Quartz & Amethyst
Animals (to cure illness)	Rose Quartz & Rock Crystal
Anorexia	Rhodochrosite & Rose Quartz
Anxiety	Rock Crystal & Tiger Eye
Arthritis	Mother of Pearl & Carnelian Also copper & Magnets
Asthma	Amber & Rose Quartz

B

Backache	Blue Agate & Hematite
Bad Temper	Blue Tiger Eye & Green Aventurine
Baldness	Aquamarine & Rock Crystal
Bladder	Jade & Red Jasper
Bleeding	Bloodstone & Carnelian
Blood Circulation	Sodalite & Carnelian
Blood Pressure (high)	Jade & Sodalite
Blood Pressure (low)	Sodalite & Carnelian
Brain Tonic	Amethyst & Carnelian
Breathlessness	Amber & Black Onyx
Bronchitis	Amber & Black Onyx
Bruises	Rose Quartz & Carnelian
Burns	Sodalite & Amethyst

C

Calming	Sodalite & Rock Crystal
Cancer	Red Jasper, Rock Crystal & Carnelian
Catarrh	Amber & Blue Agate
Cell Rejuvenation	Sodalite & Rhodonite
Central Nervous System	Rock Crystal & Rose Quartz
Chest Pains	Malachite & Rose Quartz

Circulation	Sodalite & Carnelian
Concentration	Carnelian & Red Jasper
Constipation	Red Jasper & Citrine
Coughs	Aquamarine & Blue Agate
Courage	Hematite & Tiger Eye
Cramp	Bloodstone & Amethyst
Creativity	Amethyst & Red Jasper
Crown Energy	Rock Crystal & Amethyst

D

Depression (to lift)	Tiger Eye, Carnelian & Hematite
Despair	Rhodonite & Carnelian
Diabetes	Rock Crystal & Red Jasper
Digestion	Citrine & Obsidian Snowflake
Dreams	Rutilated Quartz & Jade
Drunkenness	Amethyst & Tiger Eye

E

Ear Problems	Amethyst & Blue Agate
Eczema	Amethyst & Green Aventurine
Elixir of Life	Rhodonite & Sodalite
Emotional Strength	Amethyst & Rose Quartz
Energy Booster	Amethyst, Rock Crystal & Carnelian
Epilepsy	Black Onyx & Tourmaline
Eyesight	Obsidian Snowflake & Rose Quartz

F

Fainting	Amethyst & Lapis Lazuli
Fatigue	Amethyst, Rock Crystal & Carnelian
Fear	Rose Quartz & Rhodonite
Fertility	Rock Crystal, Rose Quartz & Moonstone
Fever	Carnelian & Red Jasper
Forgetfulness	Rhodonite & Unakite
Fractures	Mother of Pearl & Hematite
Frustration	Obsidian Clear & Rose Quartz

G

Gall Bladder	Red Jasper & Tiger Eye
General Tonic	Green Aventurine & Blue Agate

A Beginners Guide into Crystal Healing

Good Luck	Moonstone, Green Aventurine & Obsidian Snowflake
Grief	Red Jasper & Obsidian Clear

H

Haemorrhoids	Mother of Pearl & Obsidian Clear
Hair	Aquamarine & Rock Crystal
Happiness	Carnelian & Sodalite
Hay Fever	Amber & Tiger Eye
Headache	Rose Quartz & Hematite
Hearing	Blue Agate & Rhodonite
Heart Disease	Rock Crystal, Red Jasper & Carnelian
Hypochondria	Tiger Eye & Blue Agate

I

Imagine (a key to life)	Rose Quartz, Green Aventurine & Amethyst
Immune system	Blue Agate & Carnelian
Impotence	Rhodonite & Sodalite
Indigestion	Jasper & Citrine
Insomnia	Amethyst & Sodalite
Intestine	Mother of Pearl & Obsidian Snowflake
Intuition	Amethyst & Rock Crystal
Irritated Throat	Amber & Rhodonite
Itching	Green Aventurine & Hematite

K

Kidney	Jade & Carnelian
Knees	Mother of Pearl & Blue Agate
Knowledge	Amethyst & Rock Crystal

L

Laryngitis	Amber & Rhodonite
Laziness	Hematite & Blue Agate
Liver	Rhodonite & Jasper
Loneliness	Rhodochrosite & Amethyst
Love (potion)	Rose Quartz & Amethyst
Lungs	Fluorite & Amber

M

Melancholy	Red Jasper & Carnelian
Memory	Rhodonite & Unakite
Menopause	Moonstone & Rose Quartz
Menstrual Cycle	Carnelian & Moonstone
Migraine	Rose Quartz & Obsidian Clear
Mouth	Sodalite & Tiger Eye
Multiple Sclerosis	Red Jasper, Rock Crystal & Carnelian
Muscles	Rock Crystal & Hematite

N

Nails	Rhodochrosite & Mother of Pearl
Neck (tension)	Hematite & Rose Quartz
Negative Energy (to dispel)	Lapis Lazuli & Obsidian Snowflake
Nervousness	Rhodonite & Mother of Pearl
Neuralgia	Rose Quartz & Hematite
Nightmares	Amethyst & Rhodonite

O

Obesity	Black Onyx & Rock Crystal
Obsessions	Blue Agate & Black Onyx

P

Pain (to relieve)	Rose Quartz, Rock Crystal & Hematite
Paralysis	Amethyst & Rock Crystal
Patience	Rock Crystal & Howlite
Peace of Mind	Green Aventurine, Rose Quartz & Rhodonite
Phobias	Obsidian Clear & Rose Quartz
Pregnancy (for strength)	Hematite & Carnelian
Prosperity	Green Aventurine & Obsidian Snowflake
Protection	Tiger Eye & Obsidian Snowflake
Public Speaking	Amber & Tiger Eye

Q

Quarrelling (between Couples)	Rose Quartz, Green Aventurine & Rhodonite

A Beginners Guide into Crystal Healing

R
Red Blood Cells   Hematite & Amethyst
(to promote health)
Rejuvenator   Sodalite & Rhodonite
Reproductive System   Rose Quartz & Moonstone
Rheumatism   Mother of Pearl & Carnelian
                              Also Copper & Magnets

S
Sadness   Sodalite & Red Jasper
Scar Tissue   Rose Quartz & Rock Crystal
Sciatica   Rose Quartz & Hematite
Serenity   Rock Crystal & Rhodonite
Sexual Appetite   Rose Quartz, Amethyst & Carnelian
(to arouse & increase)
Shyness   Tiger Eye & Hematite
Sinus   Sodalite & Black Onyx
Skin Problems   Green Aventurine & Rose Quartz
Sleep   Amethyst, Rock Crystal & Rose Quartz
Smell (to improve)   Red Jasper & Tiger eye
Sores   Green Aventurine & Amethyst
Speech   Rhodonite & Blue Agate
Stamina   Amethyst, Rock Crystal & Carnelian
Stomach   Mother of Pearl & Obsidian Snowflake
Stress   Green Aventurine, Rose Quartz &
                              Rhodonite

T
Teeth   Mother of Pearl & Calcite
Tension   Rose Quartz & Carnelian
Throat   Blue Agate & Amber
Thyroid   Rhodonite & Lapis Lazuli
Tiredness   Amethyst, Rose Quartz & Carnelian
Tumours   Amethyst & Rose Quartz

U
Ulcers   Green Aventurine & Tiger Eye
Urinary System   Citrine & Jade

V
Varicose Veins	Aquamarine & Rhodonite
Vertigo	Red Jasper & Obsidian Clear
Vocal Cords	Amber, Rhodonite & Blue Agate

W
Wasting Disease	Red Jasper, Rock Crystal & Carnelian
Weak Muscles	Amethyst, Rock Crystal & Hematite
Weakness (general)	Amethyst, Rock Crystal & Hematite
Will Power	Rose Quartz, Black Onyx & Rock Crystal
Wisdom	Amethyst & Rock Crystal
Wounds	Rose Quartz & Rock Crystal

If thinking is the rocket
Then believing is the propellant
If thinking is the birth of the desire, the dream, the wish
Then believing makes the connection to the
Power that can make it all happen

Now look at things not as they are, but as they can be

You can accomplish almost anything if you 'believe' you can. We all have 'God-given' talents and abilities, if only we could learn how to use them. Keep an open mind ... for many, Crystal Healing works and as proved to be very beneficial, so discover for yourself if you can be one of those who can benefit.

And Finally ...
If you find you are interested in any more of my books, they can be found on eBay. To find my shop; log onto eBay.co.uk and click on the top right hand side ***Advanced.*** Then click on the left hand side ***By Seller*** and then enter my I.D. code ***rwwdhp2009*** and you will be in my shop. Here you will find all my books and Gemstone and Crystal gifts.

www.rosewood-gifts.co.uk

email :- **info@rosewood-gifts.co.uk**

A Beginners Guide into Crystal Healing

Power for Life
My 'Power for Life' book now contains, just in one edition, all of my twelve inspirational books. For those who can enjoy that feeling of being connected, or are just curious about Gemstones and Crystals, Astrology and Birthstone, Crystal Dowsing and Healing then these twelve 'Power for Life' series of books are ideal for you and are now reproduced here in just one volume.

An Alternative View on Crystal Healing
This book covers over 20 years of my experiences, including amazing details of how I became involved with Crystals and Crystal Healing. Be astonished by the Super 'Natural Powers' that are at work in everybody's life. Just go to Amazon and type in my name Robert W Wood D. Hp for further details. You can now either order for your 'Kindle' a copy or purchase a 'Print on Demand' copy anywhere in the world.

I regularly give inspirational talks and displays on Crystal Power. A captivating story about the world's fascination with natural gemstones and crystals and how the 'Placebo Effect' could be one explanation behind the healing power of gemstones and crystals, and now, for the first time, it's all in these books.

CPSIA information can be obtained at www.ICGtesting.com
Printed in the USA
LVOW12s2047280414

383562LV00029B/1410/P

9 780956 791344